> © **Take it easy**
> BY SANDEEP RAVIDUTT SHARMA

Table of Contents

Foreword IV

Take it easy..1

© **Take it easy**
BY SANDEEP RAVIDUTT SHARMA

Foreword

This book provides you with a list of **100 quotes** and thoughts about LIFE, churned out by my mind with the consciousness. grace and energy of **Shiva Shakti**. I'm sure if you keep reading, referring, sharing these thoughts and quotes about LIFE, you are likely to draw inspiration and develop good understanding of various perspectives and facts. Take it easy if life appears to be complex. There are simple solutions to complexities of life. Keep your mind cool and focus on what you can do in life rather than cribbing over what you could have done.

'Take it easy' mantra is the best way forward.

I sincerely hope, you will find this book amazing, interesting, rejuvenating, unique and a constant source of Inspiration.

Thank You and Happy Reading.

Take it easy

© Take it easy
BY SANDEEP RAVIDUTT SHARMA

Remove the complexity of your mind by thinking Simple. There are simple answers to all complex questions.

© Take it easy
BY SANDEEP RAVIDUTT SHARMA

© Copyright 2018 Sandeep Ravidutt Sharma - All rights reserved.
In no way is it legal to reproduce, duplicate, or transmit any part of this document in either electronic means or in printed format. Recording of this publication is strictly prohibited and any storage of this document is not allowed unless with written permission from the publisher. All rights reserved. The information provided herein is stated to be truthful and consistent, in that any liability, in terms of inattention or otherwise, by any usage or abuse of any policies, processes, or directions contained within is the solitary and utter responsibility of the recipient reader. Under no circumstances will any legal responsibility or blame be held against the author / publisher for any reparation, damages, or monetary loss due to the information herein, either directly or indirectly. The author own all copyrights.

Legal Notice:
This book is copyright protected. This is only for personal use. You cannot amend, distribute, sell, use, quote or paraphrase any part or the content within this book without the consent of the author or copyright owner. Legal action will be pursued if this is breached.

Disclaimer Notice:
Please note the information contained within this book is for motivational, educational and knowledge sharing purpose only. Every attempt has been made to provide the reader accurate, up to date and reliable complete information. No warranties of any kind are expressed or implied. Readers acknowledge that the author is not engaging in the rendering of legal, financial, medical or professional advice. By reading this document, the reader agrees that under no circumstances the author / publisher is responsible for any losses, direct or indirect, which are incurred as a result of the use of information contained within this document, including, but not limited to errors, omissions, or inaccuracies.

If you have further questions, contact on **Tel: +919969256731**
Email: sandeepraviduttsharma@gmail.com

© **Take it easy**
BY SANDEEP RAVIDUTT SHARMA

Dedication

This book is dedicated to **Shiva Shakti** - the epitome of love. **Lord Shiva** is pure consciousness symbolising the masculine principle. **Goddess Shakti** symbolises the active feminine energy of **Shiva** and is synonymously identified with **Tripura Sundari, Sati** or **Parvati**.
These primal principles are also called as **PURUSHA** representing consciousness and **PRAKRITI** denoting the nature. Shiva and Shakti are manifestations of the all-in-one divine consciousness. Shiva is the paternal love of God that gives us consciousness, knowledge and clarity. Shakti is the motherly love of God that showers warmth, care and ensures our protection. Shiva and Shakti exist within each of us as the masculine and feminine energy.

To please **Shiva Shakti** praying for the well being, love, happiness, strength, positive energy and success of my readers in their life, I hereby recite the following mantra...
"**Sarva Mangala Mangalye Shive Sarvartha Sadhike Sharanye Tryambake Gauri Narayani Namostute**"

© Take it easy
BY SANDEEP RAVIDUTT SHARMA

A request with a smile can never go unanswered.

© Take it easy
BY SANDEEP RAVIDUTT SHARMA

Talking about jealousy fuels it further. Attract positive thoughts and jealousy is no more.

© **Take it easy**
BY SANDEEP RAVIDUTT SHARMA

Happiness is more valuable than Gold. You can't buy or steal happiness.

If you are expecting happiness, wait is natural. Have patience, and happiness is about to reach you.

Pure thoughts emanating from a strong mind and kind heart can attract the best of the world.

© **Take it easy**
BY SANDEEP RAVIDUTT SHARMA

Trust is the key to sound human relationship.

Start your day with a firm commitment to achieve what you have decided. Have faith in your dreams and efforts.

© **Take it easy**
BY SANDEEP RAVIDUTT SHARMA

Promise only when you can deliver.

When you practice the virtue of forgiveness, your soul is purified and you enjoy bliss of God.

© **Take it easy**
BY SANDEEP RAVIDUTT SHARMA

What you do today will make your tomorrow.

© **Take it easy**
BY SANDEEP RAVIDUTT SHARMA

Those who plan well are at ease with failure as they have Plan B in place.

© **Take it easy**
BY SANDEEP RAVIDUTT SHARMA

The amazing world makes you happy. Your smiling face makes the world amazing.

© **Take it easy**
BY SANDEEP RAVIDUTT SHARMA

Acquire knowledge, gain wisdom and keep patience. Someday you will be in a position to influence the influencers.

© Take it easy
BY SANDEEP RAVIDUTT SHARMA

Happiness is a state of mind. At times you may feel happy by the sight of Golden leaves. And other times even if someone presents you the real Gold, you may dislike it and may remain unhappy.

© Take it easy
BY SANDEEP RAVIDUTT SHARMA

Those who spend more than what they earn are playing with their happiness and lives. Focus on increasing your earnings if you can't do much about your expenses.

© **Take it easy**
BY SANDEEP RAVIDUTT SHARMA

Kindness is not a one time act but a regular show where the characters keep changing but the theme remains forever.

If failure becomes a habit, it means you are not trying enough to win and has already accepted defeat before you are on the field. Keep Going with full focus and avoid past mistakes.

It's easy to give excuses than perform. But remember that's not something which the achievers do.

Happiness is a state of mind. It comes to you automatically as and when you learn and start sharing your love, thoughts, wealth, peace of mind with others who have got less of these pearls. These persons may or may not be related to you.

© Take it easy
BY SANDEEP RAVIDUTT SHARMA

Drive fast only when you are in the race else enjoy the journey.

Those who make others happy even in their dreams cannot be cruel or harsh in their real life. Dreams mirror your inner self.

True religion always guides you towards self-realisation and good deeds.

Dreams are the mirror of your hidden aspirations and unfinished agenda of your subconscious mind. Not everything which you see in your dreams you may like to turn into reality. Remember only those dreams which can motivate you in the real world. Forget those dreams which may depress you.

© Take it easy
BY SANDEEP RAVIDUTT SHARMA

It's easy to give excuses when you fail. It's much more easier to accept your failure as you don't have to weave a reason.

© Take it easy
BY SANDEEP RAVIDUTT SHARMA

Trust is a way of life and not something selective. Every day we trust so many people without even knowing them. You don't even know who drives your metro, person who delivers your newspaper, one who makes your coffee in a restaurant, who is behind the projector in a cinema hall and many more such invisible hands who never breaches your trust. Trust is universal.

© **Take it easy**
BY SANDEEP RAVIDUTT SHARMA

Analyse your failure and promise your self not to repeat those mistakes again.

Words will be words no matter whether you speak aloud or in normal tone but remember the context and impact of those words on the listener would be different each time. Choose the right words and proper tone matching the context else people would either misunderstand you or take you lightly.

© **Take it easy**
BY SANDEEP RAVIDUTT SHARMA

Don't just wish but act to fulfill them.

Happiness is rechargeable with your Smile at no cost.

© Take it easy
BY SANDEEP RAVIDUTT SHARMA

Live this golden moment instead of running after Gold.

Don't hide what you like. Expressing your likeness can pave the path of your happiness.

© **Take it easy**
BY SANDEEP RAVIDUTT SHARMA

Don't knock the door with expression of the frown. Smile and the door of opportunity opens for you.

Embrace positivity and you have got the key to the door of happiness.

Difficulties in life leads to innovative solutions.

© **Take it easy**
BY SANDEEP RAVIDUTT SHARMA

Act responsibly not because you want to show the world but to fulfill your self-commitment.

© **Take it easy**
BY SANDEEP RAVIDUTT SHARMA

Status can never be bigger than man.

Kindness is never out of stock if your heart pays for it.

© **Take it easy**
BY SANDEEP RAVIDUTT SHARMA

Winners and Losers enter the competition from the same door but only achievers are called for felicitation.

© **Take it easy**
BY SANDEEP RAVIDUTT SHARMA

Hats off to those who live for others.

Desire something, visualize the fulfillment and actually execute the plan to achieve.

© Take it easy
BY SANDEEP RAVIDUTT SHARMA

It's easy to walk away from any unfavorable situation but it needs an iron heart to absorb worst expression and still hope and strive hard for an amicable solution.

© **Take it easy**
BY SANDEEP RAVIDUTT SHARMA

Let's continue the celebration of life. Whether you lose or win doesn't make much of a difference.

© **Take it easy**
BY SANDEEP RAVIDUTT SHARMA

Harsh words can upset many and at times may work for some as a wake up call about where they are going wrong. Parents use such words sometimes without any ill intention to put their child on the right track.

Dreams become reality only when it is backed by action.

© **Take it easy**
BY SANDEEP RAVIDUTT SHARMA

Forget things which you did in the past. It's time to either do things differently or do altogether different things which can shape your future. Remember the Creator has allotted you a fixed time slot. Make the most out of your life.

© Take it easy
BY SANDEEP RAVIDUTT SHARMA

Trust never rust even with passage of time for strong characters.

It's better to believe in God rather than just believe in human.

© **Take it easy**
BY SANDEEP RAVIDUTT SHARMA

Those who postpone things are likely to succeed tomorrow. And everyone knows, tomorrow never comes. Do things now if you want to succeed.

© **Take it easy**
BY SANDEEP RAVIDUTT SHARMA

Words full of wisdom and respect opens the door of prosperity and friendship.

© Take it easy
BY SANDEEP RAVIDUTT SHARMA

VOW ensures WOW. You can hear thousands of your fans screaming WOW...only when you take and fulfill your VOW to decimate defeat and emerge as a winner.

© **Take it easy**
BY SANDEEP RAVIDUTT SHARMA

Those who speak out their mind are better than the ones who hold grudge and look forward to settle score.

© **Take it easy**
BY SANDEEP RAVIDUTT SHARMA

Don't run when you are supposed to walk.

Take it easy
BY SANDEEP RAVIDUTT SHARMA

Apology in words cannot heal the psychological wounds inflicted on others. Apologize from your heart, and it has an immediate effect.

© Take it easy
BY SANDEEP RAVIDUTT SHARMA

Testing times often pass out smoothly if you follow patience and persistence.

© Take it easy
BY SANDEEP RAVIDUTT SHARMA

Don't see your watch again and again when it's time to rejoice.

© **Take it easy**
BY SANDEEP RAVIDUTT SHARMA

If you are content with what you have today. Happiness is around you. If you are not satisfied then you have got an appointment with happiness for tomorrow. Tomorrow never comes. Choice is all yours.

If you are always busy, then, why will life see you even for a minute? Take out time and live your life.

© **Take it easy**
BY SANDEEP RAVIDUTT SHARMA

Dreams are unlimited and don't cost a dime. But tools and energy to convert them into reality are limited. So make the best out of your dreams by choosing the right action plan.

© Take it easy
BY SANDEEP RAVIDUTT SHARMA

Negativity and Positivity don't exist in its pure form within us and around. It's never purely Black and White. It's always grey. The proportion of black and white keeps changing depending on which way you are tilting based on your association with different characters of the world and stage of self-realisation you have reached.

Dreams mirror your inner self and hidden thoughts. Speak up your dream and you can find ways to fulfill them.

© **Take it easy**
BY SANDEEP RAVIDUTT SHARMA

Trust doesn't need any certificate. You can see it in the eye of the other.

© **Take it easy**
BY SANDEEP RAVIDUTT SHARMA

If no one accepts you then you don't have to start rejecting others as it would mean the same kind of behaviour which you dislike.

© **Take it easy**
BY SANDEEP RAVIDUTT SHARMA

Dream of heaven, even when you are stationed as gatekeeper of hell. Time will change and with your positive attitude, you may convert hell into heaven.

© Take it easy
BY SANDEEP RAVIDUTT SHARMA

Nothing is impossible for those who are determined to move even mountains.

Discard from your mind what is not yours or those thoughts which pulls you down. Your memory space is precious, and it should be reserved only for good and positive thoughts.

© **Take it easy**
BY SANDEEP RAVIDUTT SHARMA

Drive safe and slow on unexplored path.

Freedom cannot be suppressed and restricted for long. It would pour out more and make fun of the restrictions imposed. It's our nature.

> © **Take it easy**
> BY SANDEEP RAVIDUTT SHARMA

Dreams define your life destination.

© Take it easy
BY SANDEEP RAVIDUTT SHARMA

If God gives you two options... One is choosing happiness or sufferings... Second option is choosing happiness and sufferings... What's your choice?..... I would choose second option... Happiness for everyone and Sufferings for none...

If you develop likeness towards the best things in life. More such pleasant and interesting aspects of life will follow you.

Dreams can turn into reality only when you act.

© Take it easy
BY SANDEEP RAVIDUTT SHARMA

Don't hide your emotions and bother about the world. Let it flow without any interruption. Those who really care for you would understand your emotions. Those who don't care about you should anyway be ignored.

© **Take it easy**
BY SANDEEP RAVIDUTT SHARMA

Prosperity multiplies when you are Kind and Share your wealth with others.

© **Take it easy**
BY SANDEEP RAVIDUTT SHARMA

Trust is essential in all kinds of relationship.

Differences can be minimised if both the parties are willing to listen.

© Take it easy
BY SANDEEP RAVIDUTT SHARMA

Spend time with people who like you and ignore the rest.

Hatred of any kind is the first challenge you face on the path to embrace Love.

© Take it easy
BY SANDEEP RAVIDUTT SHARMA

Don't judge a person in haste, you may have to repent sometimes when you know the full facts.

Stay committed to your dreams by staying awake with your efforts and determination.

© Take it easy
BY SANDEEP RAVIDUTT SHARMA

When you appear to be failing and your heart is sinking. Suddenly you woke up and realise it was just a bad dream. When we can't even like failing in our dreams, just imagine the experience of a real-world failure can be quite depressing. Treat every failure as a lesson learned in your life. Don't get upset for too long.

Teachings of Guru can guide you on the path of redemption. No one can achieve enlightenment on your behalf. Be ready to redeem your soul and attain enlightenment through Devotion, Karma or Meditation.

Desires fuel our quest to scale the highest summit of our life. Control your desires if those are likely to thrown you from the peak.

© Take it easy
BY SANDEEP RAVIDUTT SHARMA

Stones make as well as break structures. It all depends on who holds them and with what intention, either wanting to build or cause harm.

© Take it easy
BY SANDEEP RAVIDUTT SHARMA

Let the world laugh at you. Remember if you are putting in sincere efforts and have got a positive attitude, you will have the last laugh.

© **Take it easy**
BY SANDEEP RAVIDUTT SHARMA

The world is always amazing for those who live in the present.

> © **Take it easy**
> BY SANDEEP RAVIDUTT SHARMA

The destination is within reach, for those who are running in its direction.

© Take it easy
BY SANDEEP RAVIDUTT SHARMA

If everyone in the family starts screaming...It's my life...then it won't be a family anymore. You may have to collaborate with some adjustments here and there. And very well say... It's our life.

© **Take it easy**
BY SANDEEP RAVIDUTT SHARMA

Remove the cobwebs of ignorance or arrogance. Condition your mind to gain insight and have better understanding.

© **Take it easy**
BY SANDEEP RAVIDUTT SHARMA

Those who stand up to protect rights of others are the real gems of our civilization.

© Take it easy
BY SANDEEP RAVIDUTT SHARMA

Speak up your mind without any hesitation and fear. People listen only to those who are courageous and kind.

Don't sleep when it's time to take action and pursue your goals. Time never revisits anyone.

Don't run without any purpose. It's better to meditate and discover own self.

© **Take it easy**
BY SANDEEP RAVIDUTT SHARMA

What applies today may not be valid tomorrow, so get ready to embrace the change.

© Take it easy
BY SANDEEP RAVIDUTT SHARMA

Get ready to live your dreams through your hard work, determination and passion to lead and win.

Nothing gets destroyed nor gets created in this world. Only things are converted from one form to another. Convert your positive affirmations into actions.

© **Take it easy**
BY SANDEEP RAVIDUTT SHARMA

Wait can be endless if you are at the right place but at the wrong time.

© **Take it easy**
BY SANDEEP RAVIDUTT SHARMA

Progressive steps can only appear in one direction. Follow them in time and you are close to prosperity.

© Take it easy
BY SANDEEP RAVIDUTT SHARMA

Meaningful dialogue needs attention of both the speaker and the listener.

© Take it easy
BY SANDEEP RAVIDUTT SHARMA

Happy mind creates the wonderful world.

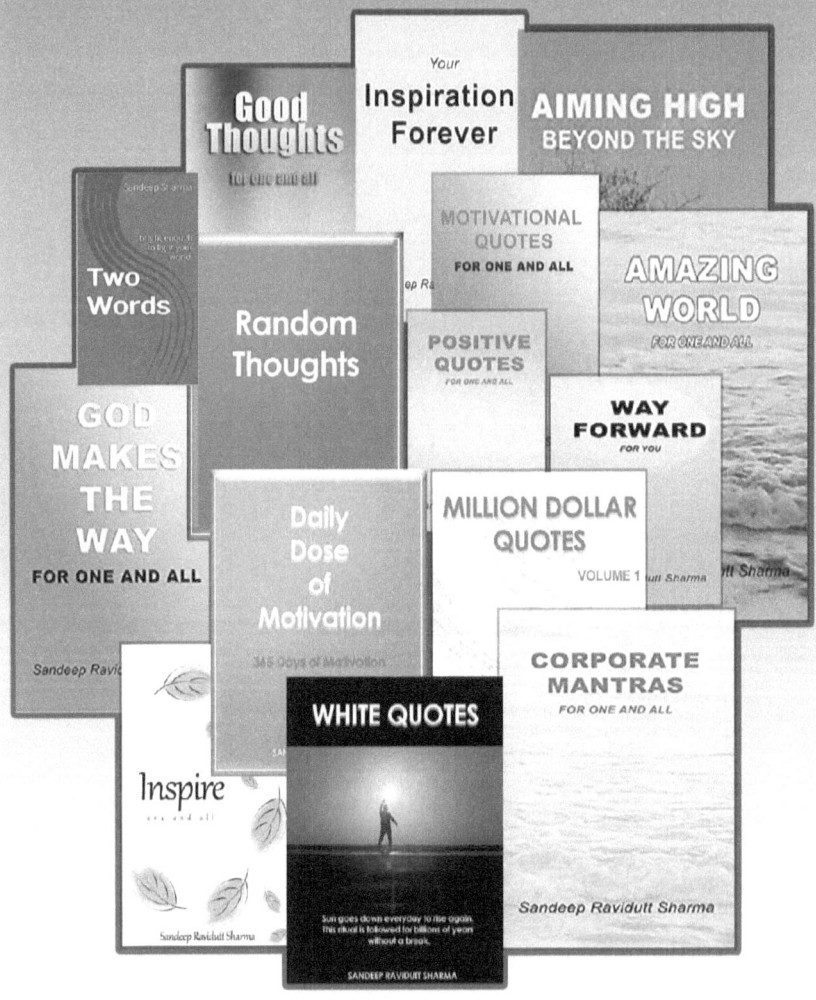

www.ingramcontent.com/pod-product-compliance
Lightning Source LLC
Chambersburg PA
CBHW031440210526
45464CB00005B/2276